I Wonder W

Countries Fly Flags

and Other Questions About People and Places

Philip Steele

Kingfisher

KINGFISHER
An imprint of Larousse plc
Elsley House, 24-30 Great Titchfield Street
London, W1P 7AD

First published by Kingfisher 1995
(hb) 10 9 8 7 6 5 4 3 2 1
(pb) 10 9 8 7 6 5 4 3 2 1
Copyright © Larousse plc 1995

A CIP catalogue record for this book is available from the
British Library

ISBN 1 85697 331 X (hb)
     1 85697 378 6 (pb)

Phototypeset by Tradespools Ltd, Frome, Somerset
Printed and bound in Italy

Series editor: Jackie Gaff
Series designer: David West Children's Books
Author: Philip Steele
Consultant: Keith Lye
Editors: Claire Llewellyn, Clare Oliver
Art editor: Christina Fraser
Picture researcher: Amanda Francis
Cover illustrations: Ruby Green, cartoons by Tony Kenyon
   (BL Kearley)
Illustrations: Peter Dennis (Linda Rogers Associates) 4-5,
   20-21, 30-31; Chris Forsey 8-9, 12-13, 17 tr, 24-25,
   26-27, 28-29; Terry Gabbey (AFA) 22-23; Luigi
   Galante (Virgil Pomfret
   Agency) 10-11, 14-15;
   Maureen Hallahan
   (BL Kearley) lettering
   8-9; Tony Kenyon
   (BL Kearley) all cartoons;
   Angus McBride (Linden
   Artists) 16-17; Nicki
   Palin 6-7, 18-19.

CONTENTS

4 What is a country?

5 Why do countries fly flags?

6 Which country has the most people?

7 Which is the biggest country?

7 Where is there land, but no countries?

8 How many countries are there?

10 Which city is above the clouds?

11 Why do Venetians walk on water?

11 Which is the world's biggest city?

12 Who writes with a paintbrush?

12 Who reads back-to-front?

13 Which country speaks over 800 languages?

14 Who lives in a longhouse?

15 Where do gardens grow on rivers?

15 How do you keep cosy in the Gobi?

16 Which is the oldest dish on the menu?

17 Who eats shells, butterflies and little worms?

17 Where does it take all afternoon to have a cup of tea?

18 Where do women wear bowler hats?

18 Where do men wear skirts?

19 Which dress has no stitches?

20 Who wears bank-notes at her wedding?

21 Where are children made kings and queens?

21 Who sticks out their tongue to say 'hello'?

22 Where do children watch shadows?

23 Who makes pictures from sand?

23 Which dancers snap their fingers?

24 Where are wheatfields bigger than countries?

25 Where does chocolate grow on trees?

25 Which country has more sheep than people?

26 Who rides on a snowmobile?

27 Where do you park your bike in China?

27 Who paints pictures on trucks?

28 Why do people race camels?

29 Which is the world's most popular sport?

30 Where do elephants glow in the dark?

30 When do people eat green food?

31 When is the Day of the Dead?

32 Index

What is a country?

A country is an independent land with its own government. The government runs the country, and makes laws which the people must keep. A country has its own name, and its borders are normally agreed by other countries around the world.

● Each country has its own money, called its currency, with its own style of coins and bank-notes. There are roubles in Russia and francs in France.

● All countries have their own stamps, which often carry a picture of the country's ruler. Some stamps show a country's wildlife, or mark an important discovery.

● People wave their national flags at parades, sports events and celebrations.

CHINA

BRAZIL

SWEDEN

GREECE

GERMANY

ISRAEL

Why do countries fly flags?

Every country has its own flag, which is a sort of national badge. Each flag is different. Its design may include coloured stripes, star and sun patterns, or religious signs such as crosses or crescents. Flags are flown on special occasions, as a symbol of a country and its people.

● Every country has its own special song called a national anthem. It is sung to show respect for a country and its history.

SUDAN

AUSTRALIA

UNITED KINGDOM

CANADA

TURKEY

ARGENTINA

SOUTH KOREA

JAMAICA

AUSTRIA

Which country has the most people?

Well over a billion people live in China, and about 48,000 new babies are born there every day. You'd think that meant a lot of birthdays, but in China everyone celebrates their birthday at the same time – the Chinese New Year!

• Chinese New Year is celebrated by Chinese people all over the world in late January or early February. There are spectacular street processions.

HAPPY BIRTHDAY

• The world's biggest-ever birthday party was on July 4, 1991. It celebrated the birthday not of a person but of two countries – the USA and Canada. Over 75,000 people turned up!

Which is the biggest country?

Russia is so big that it takes eight days to cross it by train! As children set off for school in the city of Moscow in the west, others are already going home in the eastern port of Vladivostok.

MOSCOW

VLADIVOSTOK

Where is there land, but no countries?

The vast frozen land around the South Pole is called Antarctica. It is not a country – it has no people, no government and no flag. Many countries have signed an agreement, promising to keep Antarctica as a wilderness for scientists to study.

● Nobody lives in Antarctica except for a few hundred scientists, who go there to study rocks, the weather, and the plant and animal life.

How many countries are there?

There are about 190 independent countries in the world, but the number changes from year to year. This is because new countries are sometimes made, or two countries may join together, as East and West Germany did in 1990.

CANADA

UNITED STATES

ATLANTIC OCEAN

MEXICO

PACIFIC OCEAN

CAPE VERD

ST CHRISTOPHER & NEVIS

ST LUCIA

GRENADA

VENEZUELA

COLOMBIA

GUYANA

SURINAM

PERU

BRAZIL

BOLIVIA

PARAGUAY

CHILE

ARGENTINA

URUGUAY

1 Guatemala
2 Belize
3 El Salvador
4 Honduras
5 Nicaragua
6 Costa Rica
7 Panama
8 Cuba
9 Bahamas
10 Jamaica
11 Haiti
12 Dominican Republic
13 Antigua & Barbuda
14 Dominica
15 Barbados
16 St Vincent & Grenadines
17 Trinidad & Tobago
18 Ecuador
19 Ireland
20 United Kingdom
21 Belgium
22 Netherlands
23 Luxembourg

24 Switzerland
25 Liechtenstein
26 San Marino
27 Vatican City
28 Italy
29 Monaco
30 Andorra
31 Denmark
32 Estonia
33 Latvia
34 Lithuania
35 Czech Republic
36 Austria
37 Slovakia
38 Hungary
39 Slovenia
40 Croatia
41 Bosnia & Herzogovina
42 Yugoslavia
43 Macedonia
44 Albania
45 Greece
46 Bulgaria
47 Moldova

48 Malta
49 Cyprus
50 Lebanon
51 Israel
52 Jordan
53 Armenia
54 Azerbaijan
55 Kuwait
56 Bahrain
57 Qatar
58 United Arab Emirates

- Some small Pacific island countries are not shown on this map: Fiji, Kiribati, Marshall Islands, Federated States of Micronesia, Nauru, Palau, Tonga, Tuvalu and Western Samoa.

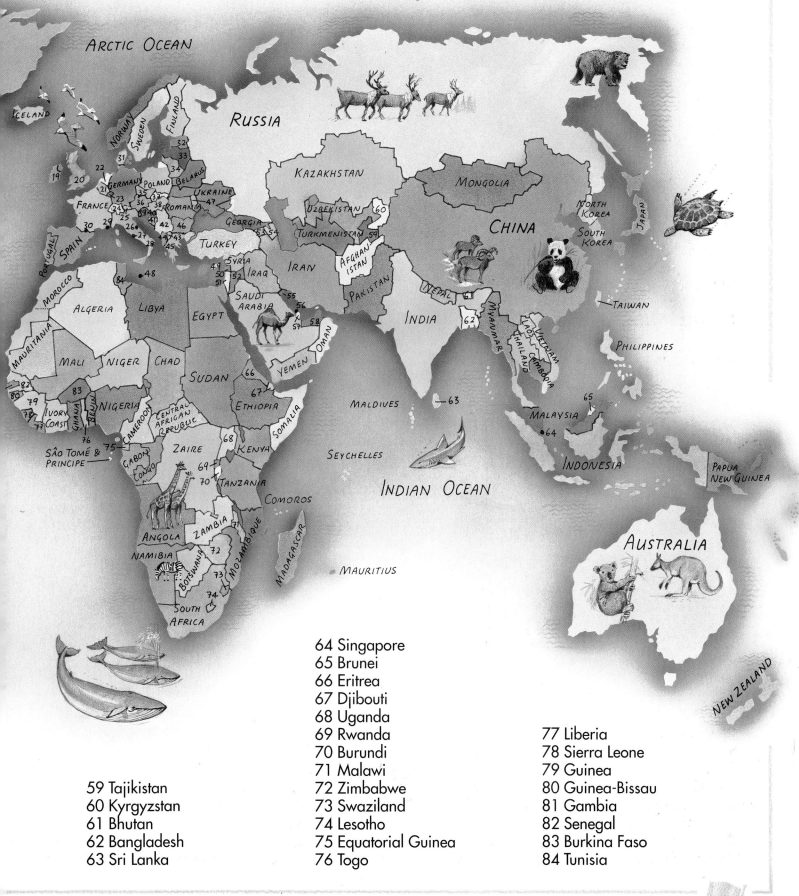

ARCTIC OCEAN

ICELAND

NORWAY
SWEDEN
FINLAND

RUSSIA

22
31
32
33
34
19 20
GERMANY POLAND BELARUS
21
FRANCE 23 35 37 UKRAINE
24 36 38 ROMANIA 47
30 29 25 39 40
41 42 46
26 GEORGIA
27 44 43
28 45
TURKEY 53 54

KAZAKHSTAN

UZBEKISTAN 60
TURKMENISTAN 59

MONGOLIA

NORTH KOREA

CHINA

JAPAN

SOUTH KOREA

PORTUGAL
SPAIN
MOROCCO
ALGERIA
LIBYA
EGYPT

84 • 48
49
SYRIA 50
52 51 IRAQ
IRAN
AFGHANISTAN
PAKISTAN
NEPAL 61
INDIA 62

TAIWAN

SAUDI ARABIA
• 55
56
57 58
OMAN
YEMEN

PHILIPPINES

MYANMAR
LAOS
THAILAND
VIETNAM
CAMBODIA

MAURITANIA
MALI
NIGER
CHAD
SUDAN
66
ETHIOPIA 67
SOMALIA

MALDIVES
— 63

MALAYSIA 65
• 64

82
80 83
79 NIGERIA
78 IVORY 76 CAMEROON
77 COAST GHANA BENIN
CENTRAL AFRICAN REPUBLIC
68
KENYA

SEYCHELLES

INDONESIA

PAPUA NEW GUINEA

SÃO TOMÉ & PRINCIPE
75
GABON
CONGO
ZAIRE
69
70 TANZANIA

INDIAN OCEAN

COMOROS

ANGOLA
ZAMBIA 71
72
NAMIBIA
BOTSWANA
73
MOZAMBIQUE
MADAGASCAR

MAURITIUS

AUSTRALIA

74
SOUTH AFRICA

NEW ZEALAND

64 Singapore
65 Brunei
66 Eritrea
67 Djibouti
68 Uganda
69 Rwanda
70 Burundi
71 Malawi
72 Zimbabwe
73 Swaziland
74 Lesotho
75 Equatorial Guinea
76 Togo

77 Liberia
78 Sierra Leone
79 Guinea
80 Guinea-Bissau
81 Gambia
82 Senegal
83 Burkina Faso
84 Tunisia

59 Tajikistan
60 Kyrgyzstan
61 Bhutan
62 Bangladesh
63 Sri Lanka

9

Which city is above the clouds?

The city of Lhasa is in Tibet, a part of China. It is built near the edge of the Himalayas, the world's highest mountains. Lhasa is so high that it's often covered by clouds, which blanket the city in a thick wet mist!

● Some people call Tibet the Roof of the World, because it so high up in the mountains.

Why do Venetians walk on water?

The Italian city of Venice is built on dozens of tiny islands in a sheltered lagoon near the sea. In between the islands are canals, which form the main 'streets' of the city. To get from one part of Venice to another, you don't take a bus or a train – you catch a motor boat or a gondola.

● A country's capital city is where the government works. Washington DC is the capital of the USA. The President lives there, in the White House.

● You have to climb 1,000 steps to reach the Potala Palace, which towers above the streets of Lhasa. It's very grand – even its roofs are made of gold!

Which is the world's biggest city?

Over 21 million people live in Mexico's capital. Mexico City is already home to more people than live in the whole of Australia, and it's growing fast!

Who writes with a paintbrush?

In China and Japan, handwriting can be an art. Instead of dashing something off with a pen, people sometimes paint words slowly and beautifully with a brush and ink. Artists often frame their work, and hang it on the wall just like a picture.

● About 50,000 different symbols may be used to write Chinese. Luckily, school children only have to learn about 5,000 of them.

● The art of beautiful handwriting is called calligraphy. Japanese children learn calligraphy at school.

Who reads back-to-front?

To read a book in Arabic or Hebrew, you have to work from right to left. So if this book were in Arabic, the first page would be where the index is now.

Which country speaks over 800 languages?

Papua New Guinea is a land of many languages. Most of the people live in small villages, deep in the rainforest or high up in the misty mountains. Some are so cut off from each other that their languages are quite different.

● In many areas of Papua New Guinea, people can only talk to each other through a translator.

● Around 5,000 languages are spoken around the world. Here are just a few ways to say "hello".

Jambo! Namaste! ¡Hola! Czesc! Dag!

Swahili Hindi Spanish Polish Dutch

● There's a place in New Zealand with 85 letters in its name. And there's another in France with just one!

Taumatawhakatangihangakoauauotamateaturipukakapikimaungahoronukupokaiwhenuakitanatahu

Who lives in a longhouse?

On the tropical island of Borneo, some people live in long, airy buildings, which are made of wood and bamboo, and are raised on stilts. These longhouses are home to dozens of different families, each with their own room.

● As many as 100 families may share the same longhouse.

● Tower blocks are another way of squeezing a lot of homes into a small space. You find them in big towns and cities.

Where do gardens grow on rivers?

In the Netherlands, many people live on barges moored on the country's canals. Boat-owners don't have gardens, of course, but some of them grow flowers on the roof!

How do you keep cosy in the Gobi?

The Gobi Desert is in Mongolia in northern Asia and its winters are icy cold. Some shepherds and their families travel around the desert, living in thick, felt tents called yurts, which keep out the hot sun or the freezing cold.

Which is the oldest dish on the menu?

● All over the world, people pound grains such as maize to make flour for their pancakes.

Pancakes may be the oldest dish of all. Even Stone Age people baked them! The basic recipe – milk, eggs and flour – is the same the world over, but the kind of flour changes from place to place. Pancakes can be made using flour from potatoes, maize, wheat or oats.

● In different parts of the world you might find almost anything on your plate – from crunchy insects or chewy snails, to snakes, guinea pigs, or even sheep's eyes!

16

Who eats shells, butterflies and little worms?

● Table manners change from place to place. The British think you're rude if you put your elbows on the table, while the French think it's perfectly all right!

We do! These are all types of pasta – their Italian names are conchiglie (shells), farfalle (butterflies) and vermicelli (little worms). Pasta is a dough made from flour and water, which is cut into shapes and cooked. It's simply delicious served with a tasty sauce and a sprinkling of cheese.

Vermicelli

Farfalle

Conchiglie

● Pasta dough comes in over 100 shapes and sizes. It's cut into stars, shells, snail shapes, and all the letters of the alphabet.

Where does it take all afternoon to have a cup of tea?

In Japan there's a special ancient tea ceremony called chanoyu. The tea is made so slowly, and sipped so carefully, that it really does take hours. It's not a good idea to turn up to the ceremony feeling thirsty!

Where do women wear bowler hats?

In the Andes Mountains of South America, many of the women wear round bowler hats. The hat has become a part of their traditional dress, along with full skirts and brilliantly-coloured llama-wool shawls and ponchos.

• Lake Titicaca, up in the Andes, is the highest lake in the world. The people there use reed boats to travel between islands.

• Bowler hats were first made for men, not women! British businessmen have worn them to work for over 100 years.

Where do men wear skirts?

On special occasions in the Highlands of Scotland, it's traditional for men to wear kilts. These pleated skirts are made of a checked woollen cloth called tartan. Kilts are warm, but they only come down to the knee, so they are worn with a pair of long, woolly socks.

Which dress has no stitches?

The Indian sari is a simple length of cloth, which wraps neatly around a woman's body. It has no stitching, buttons or zips and its design hasn't really changed for hundreds of years. Saris are made of bright cottons or shimmering silks, and on a hot day they are delightfully cool and comfortable to wear.

● People who live in desert countries traditionally wear long robes and head cloths to protect them from the heat and dust. In Arctic countries people wrap up warmly in fur-lined anoraks and parkas.

● In Scotland, each family group has its own tartan, with a particular pattern and colour.

Who wears bank-notes at their wedding?

At a Greek or Turkish wedding, the guests don't take the bride and groom gifts – they give them money instead. At the wedding party, guests pin bank-notes all over the couple's clothes. Often there is so much money that it completely covers their clothes!

● On the island of Madagascar, a man makes a speech to his bride-to-be before she'll marry him. If the speech is no good, he pays a fine and starts again!

● Hindu brides decorate their skin with beautiful, lacey patterns for their wedding day. They use a reddish-brown dye called henna.

Where are children made kings and queens?

On January 6th, French families enjoy a special dinner together. At the end of the meal, the children eat slices of a flat almond pie called a galette. In one of the slices a charm is hidden, and whoever finds it is crowned king or queen for the night.

● Three kings from the East are said to have visited the two-week-old baby Jesus on January 6th.

Who sticks out their tongue to say 'hello'?

One of the customs of the Maori people of New Zealand is to welcome important guests by staring at them fiercely, and sticking out their tongues – not something you should try unless you're a Maori!

Where do children watch shadows?

Shadow puppet shows are enjoyed by people all over the world. On the Indonesian island of Java, the audience sits on both sides of a cloth screen. One side watches the puppets while the other sees the shadows dance, as if by magic!

● Javanese puppets are made of painted leather. The puppeteer moves them with wires or rods.

● In a Vietnamese water puppet show, the story is acted out on the surface of a lake. It can't be much fun for the puppeteers – they have to stand in the water.

Who makes pictures from sand?

The Navajo people of the southwestern United States create beautiful pictures with grains of coloured sand. The pictures are made on the ground for special ceremonies. But these works of art don't last long – they are destroyed afterwards!

● Some sand pictures are said to have healing powers and are large enough for someone ill to sit in the middle of them.

● In Switzerland, cow herders used to play alpenhorns – long wooden horns which echoed from one mountain to another.

Which dancers snap their fingers?

Flamenco dancing comes from southern Spain. Proud-looking dancers toss their heads and snap their fingers, as they stamp and whirl to the music of a Spanish guitar.

Where are wheatfields bigger than countries?

The rolling grasslands of Canada and the USA are planted with wheat as far as the eye can see. One Canadian wheatfield was so big, it was double the size of the European country, San Marino!

● Huge combine harvesters have to work in teams to harvest the gigantic wheatfields.

● More people eat rice than wheat. Rice plants need to stand in water, and are grown on flooded land called paddy fields.

Where does chocolate grow on trees?

Chocolate is made from the seeds of the cacao tree. Sadly, the trees don't grow everywhere – just in the hot, wet parts of South America, southeast Asia and West Africa.

Which country has more sheep than people?

● In Thailand, coconut farmers train monkeys to harvest their crop. The monkeys scamper up the trunks of the palm trees and throw down the fruits.

Although there are more than 17 million people in Australia, most live around the coast. In the centre people run enormous sheep farms. At the last count, there were 147 million sheep – nearly nine times the number of people!

Who rides on a snowmobile?

Many of the people who live in icy Alaska and northern Canada travel across the frozen snow on powerful sleds called snowmobiles. Not long ago, sleds were pulled by husky dogs, but nowadays these are only raced for fun.

• A dog team can pull a sled about 80 kilometres in a day. A snowmobile covers that in an hour!

• Trains in Tokyo, Japan, are so crowded that railway staff called crushers have to push in the passengers while the doors close.

• Fishermen in Portugal paint 'magic' eyes on their boats to watch over them at sea and bring them safely to harbour.

Where do you park your bike in China?

There are millions and millions of people in China, and millions and millions of bikes! So all Chinese cities have huge cycle parks, where an attendant gives your bike a number, and helps you to find it again later.

Who paints pictures on trucks?

The truck drivers of Afghanistan are very proud of their trucks. They paint holy pictures all over them, covering every last centimetre in bright, colourful patterns. Even the wheel nuts are painted different colours.

● The Afghans may drape their trucks with silver chains, and even stick on ring-pulls from drink cans as decorations.

Why do people race camels?

One-humped camels are so sturdy and fast that in hot desert areas they are ridden like racehorses. The races are very popular in Saudi Arabia, and large crowds cheer the camels as they speed across desert racetracks.

● Dromedaries can race at over 20 kilometres an hour – faster than two-humped camels.

● People have been known to race all sorts and sizes of animal – from ostriches to snails!

• The world's fastest ball game is called pelota. The ball is hurled from a wicker scoop at the speed of an express train.

Which is the world's most popular sport?

Footballs are kicked about in more than 160 countries around the world. The game is played by thousands of people, in playgrounds, parks, streets and, of course, football grounds.

• The earliest football-like game was called zuqiu. It was played 2,400 years ago in Ancient China.

Where do elephants glow in the dark?

For the Sri Lankan festival of the Esala Perahera, elephants are decorated with beautiful hangings and strings of electric lights. More than 50 elephants take part in a night-time procession, along with thousands of drummers and dancers, who crack whips and wave colourful banners.

● The leprechaun of Irish folktales is a little green man. The green shamrock is Ireland's national flower.

When do people eat green food?

Saint Patrick is the patron saint of Ireland, and green is the country's national colour. Saint Patrick's Day falls on March 17th, and for Irish people everywhere it's a time of wild celebration. Some people even dye party food and drink green!

When is the Day of the Dead?

The Day of the Dead is a Mexican holiday which takes place every year on November 2nd, All Soul's Day. People remember dead friends and relatives by taking flowers and candles to their graves, and having picnics there.

● Brightly painted papier-mâché skeletons are made for the Day of the Dead celebrations.

● February is carnival time in many countries, with glittering parades and music.

● The Esala Perahera procession takes place in Kandy, Sri Lanka, at the time of the July full moon.

Index

A

Afghanistan 9, 27
Alaska 26
Andes 18
Antarctica 7
Australia 9, 11, 25

B

bank-note 4,
    20 see also
    currency
Borneo 14

C

camel race 28
Canada 6, 8, 24, 26
chanoyu 17
China 6, 9, 10, 12, 27, 29
city 7, 10-11, 14, 27
clothing 18-19
country 4-5, 6-7, 8-9, 24, 29
currency 4
customs 20-21, 23

F

farming 24-25
festival 6, 30, 31
flag 4, 5, 7

flamenco 23
food 16-17, 21, 24, 25, 30
football 29
France 4, 9, 13, 17, 21

G

Germany 8, 9
government 4, 7, 11

H

home
    14-15

I

India 9, 19
Indonesia 9, 22
Ireland 8, 9, 30
Italy 8, 9, 11, 17

J

Japan 9,
    12, 17, 26
Java 22

L

language 12-13
longhouse 14

M

Madagascar 9, 20
Maori 21
Mexico 8, 11, 31
Mongolia 9, 15

N

national anthem 5

Navajo 23
Netherlands 8, 9, 15
New Zealand 9, 13, 21

P

Papua New Guinea 9, 13
Portugal 9, 26
postage stamp 4
puppet 22

R

Russia 4, 7, 9

S

sand picture 23
Scotland 18, 19
Spain 9, 13, 23
sport 4, 28-29
Sri Lanka 9, 30
Switzerland 8,
    9, 23

T

Tibet 10
Thailand 9, 25
transport 11, 15, 18, 26-27

U

USA 6, 8, 11, 23, 24

W

wedding 20
wheatfield 16, 24

Y

yurt 15